W9-BNS-822

Discovering
Cultures

Iran

Wil Mara

 **Marshall Cavendish**
Benchmark
New York

For Janaki Little

Marshall Cavendish
99 White Plains Road
Tarrytown, New York 10591-9001
www.marshallcavendish.us

Library of Congress Cataloging-in-Publication Data

Mara, Wil.
Iran / by Wil Mara.
p. cm. — (Discovering cultures)
Includes bibliographical references and index.
ISBN-13: 978-0-7614-1986-0
ISBN-10: 0-7614-1986-1
1. Iran—Juvenile literature. I. Title. II. Series.
DS254.75.M37 2006
955—dc22   2006011476

Photo Research by Candlepants Incorporated
Cover Photo: Yoshio Tomii / Super Stock

The photographs in this book are used by permission and through the courtesy of: *Corbis*: Tibor Bognar, 1; Brian A. Vikander, 8, 22, 15, 42(top left); Earl & Nazima Kowall, 10; Diego Lezama Orezzoli, 12(top left); Attar Maher/Sygma, 17; Kaveh Kazemi, 18, 26, 16, 29, 30, 31, 43(top left), 43(lower right); Dave Bartruff, 19, 14; Peter Turnley, 25(top); Arthur Thevenart, 28; Reuters, 32; Morteza Nikoubazi/Reuters, 35, 36, 37, 38, back cover; Paul Almasy, 39; Lynsey Addario, 44(top); Bettmann, 45. *Super Stock*: Kurt Scholz, 4; Catherine de Torquat, 13. *Photo Researchers Inc.*: Dr. Peter Moore, 6, 42(middle right). *Getty Images*: Robert Harding, 7; Keren Su, 11; Phil Weymouth, 12(right). *Peter Arnold Inc.*: Jeffrey L. Rotman, 9; Shehzad Noorani, 20, 21, 24, 25(lower), 43(lower left). *The Image Works*: Hideo Haga/HAGA, 34. *Index Stock*: Dave Bartruff, 44(lower).

Cover: *The Tower of Freedom, Tehran, Iran;* Title page: *An Iranian Kurd wearing a head cloth*

Map and illustrations by Ian Warpole
Book design by Virginia Pope

Printed in Malaysia
1 3 5 6 4 2

Turn the Pages...

Where in the World Is Iran?

Iran is in southwestern Asia, about 6,000 miles (9,656 kilometers) from the eastern coast of the United States. It is the second-largest country in an area of the world known as the Middle East. Saudi Arabia is the largest.

Iran is surrounded by both land and water. To the north are the Caspian Sea, plus the nations of Armenia, Azerbaijan, and Turkmenistan. Although called a "sea," the Caspian is often considered the world's largest lake, since it also has many characteristics of a lake and is about 143,250 square miles (371,000 sq km) in size. Afghanistan and Pakistan lie to the east. In the south, there is only water—the Gulf of Oman in the southeast, and the Persian Gulf in the south-west. And in the west, Iran is next to Iraq and Turkey.

Horses on the shore of the Caspian Sea

4

Map of Iran

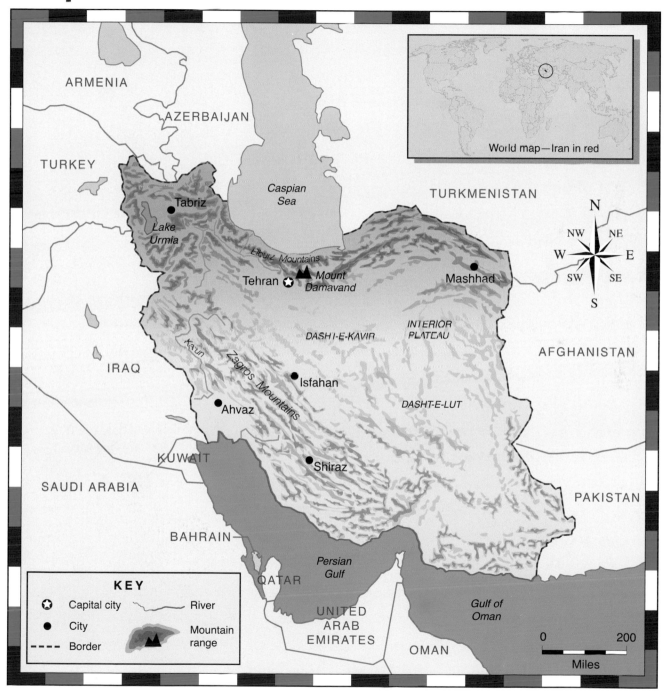

ARMENIA

AZERBAIJAN

TURKEY

Tabriz

Lake Urmia

Caspian Sea

TURKMENISTAN

Elburz Mountains

Tehran ☆ Mount Damavand

Mashhad

IRAQ

Karun

Zagros Mountains

DASHT-E-KAVIR

INTERIOR PLATEAU

AFGHANISTAN

Isfahan

DASHT-E-LUT

Ahvaz

KUWAIT

Shiraz

SAUDI ARABIA

PAKISTAN

BAHRAIN

QATAR

Persian Gulf

UNITED ARAB EMIRATES

Gulf of Oman

OMAN

World map—Iran in red

N
NW   NE
W   E
SW   SE
S

KEY

☆ Capital city   River
● City   Mountain range
---- Border

0   200
Miles

Mountains stand behind a sandy desert in northwestern Iran.

There are three main types of land in Iran: plateaus, mountains, and lowlands. A plateau is a flat area high above the level of the sea. Iran's largest plateau, called the Interior Plateau, takes up about half of the country. Most of it is empty desert. Iran has two major mountain ranges—the Elburz in the north, and the Zagros in the west. People live in the valleys of these mountains, where water runs down from the slopes and keeps the soil in good condition. The lowlands are usually found along the coast. They provide the best place for Iranian people to live. They have pleasant year-round temperatures and plenty of good land for farming.

The climate in Iran varies from place to place. In the pleasant lowland area that sits between the Elburz Mountains and the Caspian Sea, temperatures in the summer are about 85 degrees Fahrenheit (29 degrees Celsius) and 35 °F (2 °C) in the

The Elburz Mountains are one of two major mountain ranges in Iran.

winter. Humidity is low, and gentle breezes roll off the water all year long. The mountains and valleys, on the other hand, have harsh winters. Temperatures fall below freezing, and there is plenty of snow and rain. In the plateaus, it may be as pleasant as the lowlands or as cold as the valleys. Some plateau areas fall below freezing in the winter, and then reach as high as 130 °F (54 °C) in the summer. There is also almost no rainfall. This makes it impossible to grow crops.

Iran's highest mountain is Mount Damavand. It is also a *dormant* volcano, and it is nearly 19,000 feet (5,791 meters) above sea level. Iran's longest river is the Karun. It runs for 450 miles (724 km). It runs from the western slopes of the Zagros Mountains to Iran's border with Iraq. The largest lake is Urmia. It covers more than 1,750 square miles (4,532 sq km) and is located near the city of Tabriz. Urmia's water has so much salt and other minerals that fish cannot live there. This also means the water is undrinkable.

Iran's capital city is Tehran. It is located at the northwestern edge of one of Iran's largest deserts, the Dasht-e-Kavir. Tehran is the center of Iran's industry and business. It has many government buildings, offices, and factories. More than 12 million people live there. Most of them have electricity and telephones, but there is often a shortage of fresh water. Tehran also has more than forty colleges, plus several museums. Other major Iranian cities include Mashhad, which is an important manufacturing and religious area; Tabriz, which makes items that are sold to other countries; and Ahvaz, which is the main area of Iran's oil industry. Shiraz, which was the capital of Persia in the late eighteenth century, is the home to many of Iran's writers, musicians, actors, and other artists. Isfahan, Iran's third largest city, features some of the nation's most beautiful architecture. It is also one of the most popular Iranian cities for tourists.

Iran's capital city, Tehran, lies between a desert and mountains.

The Saw-Scaled Viper

The saw-scaled viper is often called "the most dangerous snake in the world." This snake is found in the dry areas of central and eastern Iran. It is always alert and highly nervous, and it is one of the few snakes reported to have actually *chased* people rather than flee.

The saw-scaled viper gets its name from the sound it makes when it coils to attack. Its tough, pointed scales rub together, making a sawing sound. It strikes over and over, injecting venom that can cause a slow and painful death. It will bury itself in the sand, with only its eyes sticking out, to wait for its prey.

What Makes Iran Iranian?

Around 1500 BCE, people in central Asia began moving into the area that is now Iran. They called this area Persia. Today, 51 percent of Iranians are descendants of these Persian people. Two other large ethnic groups in Iran are the Azeri and the Kurds. They are both closely related to the Persians. Over the last one hundred years, many people from Turkey have also moved to Iran. All of these groups, plus a few other, smaller groups, make up Iran's population.

This Iranian man wears a long scarf called a turban wound around his head.

There is one official language in Iran. It should come as no surprise that it is called Persian. It does have another name, too—Farsi. It is one of the oldest languages in the world that is still used today. Persian is spoken slightly differently in different areas of Iran. This is similar to the way

A mosque lit up at night

people in the southern United States are said to have a "Southern accent." The Iranian government has tried to create a single, national version of Persian by teaching it in the country's schools.

Iranian art is among the most beautiful in the world. Poems, for example, have been a beloved art form for centuries in Iran. Famous poets are considered to be heroes. It is not unusual to hear Iranians use lines from great poems when they talk each day! Iran is also known for the design of its buildings. *Mosques* are similar to churches—they are houses of religious worship. Many Iranian mosques

Tiles arranged in mosaics decorate the ceiling of a mosque.

Women weaving Persian rugs

are decorated with thousands of colorful tiles, creating stunning *mosaics*. Some also have Arabic calligraphy, which is a stylish form of writing. Iranian weavers make carpets, which are called "Persian rugs" by many. They are considered the best carpets in the world. No machines are used. Each carpet is made by hand, almost always by a woman, who might spend months creating just one!

In recent times, Iranian art—everything from books to paintings to movies—has called for greater social justice and equality. Young artists in Iran push for more rights for Iranian women, differences in religious beliefs, and less governmental control. Unfortunately, this is not always easy for the artists. Much of Iran's art has to be approved by the government's Ministry of Islamic Guidance before anyone can see it.

When out in public, Iranian women cover their hair and wear chadors to cover their bodies.

Women are required, by Iranian law, to cover their hair, arms, and legs, especially when they are out in public. Most Iranian women do this by wearing a *chador*, which is a long, loose robe. Boys and men usually dress much the same as Americans do. They wear cotton slacks, a dress shirt, and sometimes a jacket for important occasions. They will wear shorts and sandals when it is hot. Some Iranian males will also wear a *turban* to show their religious faith. This is a long scarf wrapped around the head.

The main religion in Iran is Islam. According to Islam, every person lives to serve God. People who follow this religion are called Muslims. They believe a man named Muhammad was the last person to whom God spoke directly. Muhammad was born in the mid-500s and died in the early 600s. Just as Christians have the Bible, Islamic people have a holy book called the *Qur'an*. Many of Iran's laws are based on Islamic beliefs. Many of the written laws have actual lines from the Qur'an.

Perfume in bottles for sale in Iran

Iran has given many things to the rest of the world. Iranians may have been the first people to use natural resources to help them farm their land. For instance, early Iranians used animals to help with farmwork, and they dug trenches to change the flow of a river in order to water crops. Iran probably was the first nation to grow spinach as a food source, and the first to figure out how to store wine in order to keep it fresh. Iranians were also among the earliest people to play the game of polo, which they called *chowgan*. They also discovered how to create perfumes from the beautiful scents of various flowers, and were the first to cultivate roses. In fact, the word "rose" is thought to have come from the Persian language.

The Poetry of Hafez

Shams-od-Din Muhammad Hafez was born in the Iranian city of Shiraz in the early 1300s. His last name, Hafez, means "memorizer of the Qur'an." He had great knowledge of the Islamic religion. He also wrote some of the most famous poetry in Iran's history. Many claim his poems can predict the future. Even today, some Iranians will open a book of Hafez's poetry, pick out a line, and use the information in that line to determine what they will do in the coming days, weeks, and months. Hafez died in 1389, and his grave site is considered a national landmark.

Living in Iran

There are two main places to live in Iran: cities and villages. Each has its own interesting features, and the people who live there have very different lifestyles.

Most people live in cities. The cities are busy because they are centers of business and spiritual life. The streets are packed with houses and apartment buildings. An ordinary day in an Iranian city is much like a day in a city in the United States.

Iranians on motorbikes stuck in a traffic jam in Tehran

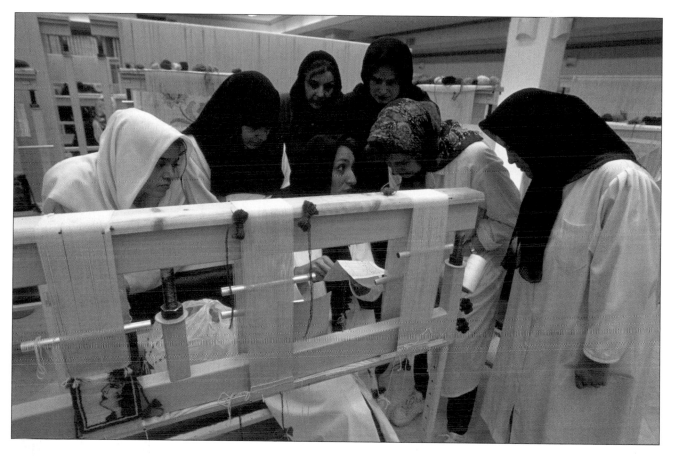

At work in a factory

Many people wake early in the morning, shower, dress, have breakfast, then head out to work. Some drive their own cars. Others walk, ride bicycles, or take the bus. People travel fast on roads in an Iranian city. Even though there are signs and traffic lights, drivers go faster than the speed limit. Some weave in between other cars as if they were playing a video game.

People have lots of different jobs in the city. There are office managers, doctors, shop owners, factory workers, teachers, and police officers. Average

This man owns a business selling nuts and dried fruits.

Iranians will start work at about 9 a.m., then stop for lunch, their main meal, around noon. They will return home around 5 p.m. The average workday is about eight hours. People who own businesses may have to work longer hours or more days.

A typical chicken and rice meal

At the end of the day, a worker returns home to a good meal. Iranians love good food. A typical meal will include rice, bread, and a variety of vegetables. Sometimes there is fish or meat as well. Yogurt is part of many meals, often mixed with fresh fruit or soda. Iranians also use a variety of tasty spices. Coriander, saffron, and mint are popular.

The end of the workday also means time to be with family. A strong family life is very important in Iran. The father is considered the head of the household. He sets the rules and often earns most of the money. The mother watches over the children, making sure they behave themselves and pay attention to important things. Many Iranian women also hold down full-time jobs, which helps keep a household running smoothly. Women are also allowed to vote in political elections, go to college, hold high-paying jobs, and seek

Family life is very important to Iranians.

powerful government positions. Women in some other Muslim societies are not allowed any of these rights.

Iranian children are allowed to play and have fun, but they are also expected to do well in school, do their chores, and show respect to others. Children go to school during the day. If they are not yet old enough for school, they might help their mothers with the daily chores. These include washing, preparing food, cleaning, and shopping. They often shop in city streets lined with tables and carts selling everything from groceries to clothing. These areas are called *bazaars*.

A woman buys fabric in a bazaar.

Farmers traveling on donkeys

People who live in villages are usually farmers. Farming is hard work. The head of the family sometimes needs help from his wife, his children, and even his neighbors. Fortunately, most of the villages are located in areas where there is enough good soil, water, and sunshine. Farmers also have animals that produce other things they can sell, such as goats for their milk or sheep for their wool. The average Iranian farmer lives in a brick-and-mud home with a wooden floor and a thatched roof. The family sleeps on the floor, often on straw mats and blankets. Most villages have electricity and clean water. They will also have a mosque, a hospital of some kind, and an elementary school.

Doogh

If you would like to try a delicious Iranian drink, doogh is a good one that is easy to make. Remember to have an adult help you, and make sure you wash your hands before and after.

Ingredients:

1 cup plain yogurt

1 tall glass carbonated mineral water

1 teaspoon dried mint

A pinch or two of salt

Beat the yogurt with a fork or whisk until it is smooth. Add the mint and the salt and continue mixing. Add the mineral water, and continue to mix gently. You can vary the amount of water/yogurt mixture to reach a desired thickness. Once everything is mixed, chill the drink in the refrigerator for about two hours. Remove from refrigerator and stir one more time. Now it is ready for drinking.

School Days

Iranians did not have a formal school system until the late nineteenth century, when they opened their first professional school. At that time, only boys went to school, and they spent much of their time studying the Qur'an. In the early 1900s, some girls' schools were also established in Tehran, but it was not until 1943 that Iran's leader, Reza Khan Pahlavi, officially said that girls could go to school,

A girl writes at her desk.

too. In addition to the Qur'an, schools began teaching many other subjects, such as mathematics, science, reading, writing, social studies, and the arts. Before these changes took place, only about 30 percent of the people could read and write. Today more than 79 percent of Iranians can read and write.

Iran's schools are similar to those in the United States. Children begin with what is called a preschool year, then go to elementary school for grades one through five. These are called their primary school years. Middle school is for grades six through eight. After that, they have four years of what Americans would consider high school, but in Iran is called secondary education. This is for grades nine through twelve. During this time an Iranian student can choose to focus on academic studies, such as literature, science, or mathematics, or job skills, such as carpentry or electronics. After their secondary education, they can go to college.

Students sing along with their teacher.

The grading system in Iran is different from the American system. In Iran, grades are based on numbers from 1 to 20. An "A" in Iran would mean a number grade of 17–20. A "B" would be 14–16.9. A "C" would be 12–13.9. And a "D" would be from 10 to 11.9. A student earning an overall grade of anything lower than a 10 would not be allowed to pass to the next higher class.

The average school day lasts about eight hours. Each lesson is about ninety minutes long. Teachers can be either men or women. The teachers do most of the talking during a lesson, although children can raise their

Performing a play in the classroom

hands to ask questions or make comments. At the end of each lesson there is a short break. Students can have drinks and snacks.

Girls pray with a religious leader at school.

Students often wear uniforms to school. Girls must wear chadors to cover everything except their hands and faces. Boys wear pants and dress shirts. Girls and boys are not taught together. They have separate classrooms. Sometimes they even have separate schools.

At noon, all students have group prayer. Most Muslims will stop to pray up to five times a day. These times are at dawn, noon, midafternoon, sunset, and before bed. Once students get home, they have to do their homework. Homework can take another two or three hours.

In the past, many children who lived far from the cities were unable to get an education. Children in villages had no way of getting to class. Also, many of them had to work on their parents' farms. They did not have much time for school. To solve this problem, the Iranian government built more schools in the villages. Today, about 78 percent of these children attend school. In the early part of the twentieth century, that number was as low as 35 percent.

The Teachings of the Qur'an

The Qur'an teaches students more than just religion. For many Iranians, the Qur'an guides them throughout their life. Children are introduced to it at a very young age and study it throughout their school days. The Qur'an is thought to create a link between people and God, who is called Allah in Islam. It also encourages them to think about who they are and how they can make themselves better. By the time students are done with school, they are expected to have learned what it means to be good citizens and good Muslims.

Just for Fun

Iranians spend plenty of time on serious matters, such as work, chores, and prayers. But that does not mean they do not know how to have fun!

One way Iranians relax is by spending time with friends and family. The average Iranian home is a place of warmth and hospitality. Many people who have visited Iran have noticed this. Sometimes twenty or thirty people gather in one house. It is filled with the sounds of music and people talking. The smell of fine cooking drifts through the air. An entire family may live in the same town, so one person's home becomes a common place for all of the relatives to visit.

Families relax in a park on the banks of a river.

Iranians also talk with friends at their local mosque, after prayers. Friday is the day of group prayer for Islam. It is similar to Sunday in Christianity. Afterward, men will gather in the mosque's courtyard and talk in one group, while women chat in another group, and the children play.

Sometimes an Iranian family will pack a basket with food and drink, roll up one of their beautiful rugs, and go to a local park for a picnic. Picnicking has become very popular in Iran. At the park, people may play board games on tables. Some games are not allowed by the Iranian government. This is because Islam forbids all forms of gambling. However, other games are still permitted, like chess—which has been traced to ancient Iran—and backgammon.

In the cities, young Iranians are a lot like young people in the United States. They hang out with their friends at shopping malls or at the movies. They talk on cell phones. Many young people have computers, so they also send e-mail to each other. Iranian youths who do not have computers can

Teenage boys hang out with friends in a local park.

Girls online at an Internet café

go to a place called an "Internet café." There they pay a fee to use a computer. Young Iranians also enjoy many video games.

Families often take trips to the beaches along the coasts. At the beaches, the weather is nice most of the year. Beach lovers play in the sand, swim in the sea, and enjoy the warmth of the sun. However, Iranian women are not allowed to

Swimming in the Caspian Sea

wear bathing suits. They must cover their bodies as much as possible, even when they are in the water. There are many beach resorts along the Caspian Sea. They not only have beautiful beaches but also comfortable hotels, fine restaurants, and places to shop.

Sports have always been popular in Iran. Many excellent athletes are Iranian, and some have been on Olympic teams. The most popular sport in Iran is soccer.

Iran (right) and Denmark fight for the ball during an international soccer game.

Most people watch it on television. Some go to stadiums to watch the games. However, women are not allowed to go to sporting events.

Iranians who live in farming villages cannot usually get to soccer stadiums or movie theaters. They spend their free time visiting friends and family. Children play soccer along the quiet dirt roads. They also invent their own games using sticks, pebbles, and anything else they can find. Sometimes a traveling group of actors and musicians may come into the village. They will put on plays, perform songs, and tell stories.

"Forty Fortunes"

"Forty Fortunes" is an ancient Iranian story. It tells of a great king whose royal treasure has been stolen. The king asks his most trusted friends to find it, but they cannot. Then he asks Ahmed to help. Ahmed is an ordinary young man, but the king thinks he has the power to see into the future. Ahmed knows this is not true, so he asks the king for forty days in which to find the treasure. The first thirty-nine days go by, and nothing happens. On the fortieth day, Ahmed gets very lucky. He finds the thieves and makes them return the treasure. Ahmed then tells the king that all of his great powers were used up, and he can do no more. The king rewards him and sends him on his way.

Let's Celebrate!

Iranians have holidays just like any other nation, but they follow a different calendar than people do in the United States. In Iran, the movements of the sun and moon decide the days and months. That means some of their holidays are on different days each year.

The two most important holidays are Nowruz and Ramadan. Nowruz is the Iranian New Year. It occurs on or very close to March 21. It is one of Iran's oldest holidays, and marks the first day of spring. The celebration lasts for thirteen days. It is considered a time of rebirth and starting over. If you have ever seen your parents perform their spring cleaning chores around this time, then you have some idea of how Iranians celebrate

Families picnicking at a Nowruz celebration

34

A girl visits a war memorial during Nowruz.

Nowruz. Rugs are removed from every room in an Iranian home, hung outside, and beaten until all dust and dirt are gone. Windows are opened to bring fresh air inside. Old clothes are either thrown out or mended.

Iranians also try to cleanse their souls and minds during Nowruz. Old friendships are started again, past fights are forgotten and forgiven. People start small fires in the streets, then jump over them to burn away bad habits and bad luck. Huge meals are prepared, and presents are given to children. Poems from great Iranian writers are read, often to provide guidance for the coming year. Most schools, businesses, and government offices are closed. Some feel the last day of Nowruz can cause bad luck. Many Iranians will leave their homes until this day is over.

A Muslim woman and her daughter view Islamic drawings at an exhibit during Ramadan.

Ramadan is a very religious holiday. It occurs at a different time each year and lasts about a month. Muslims believe that Muhammad was told the first verses of the Qur'an by an angel named Gabriel. This happened while Muhammad was wandering around the desert near the holy city of Mecca. Muslims celebrate this important event by observing Ramadan. During this time, they will not eat or drink anything while the sun is up. Before sunrise, they will eat a meal called *suhoor*. They eat again after the sun has gone down. This meal is called *iftar*. By not being allowed to eat during the day, they remember that there are some people in the world who go without food all the time.

Ramadan ends with a celebration called Eid al-Fitr. This means "Festival of the Breaking of the Fast." There will be lots of food, visits from friends and family, and more gifts for children. Everyone wears their finest clothes and decorates their homes. Muslims are also required to give something to someone poor. This is often a good meal and some new clothing. They may also give money to their local mosque.

Iran has other holidays, too. There is the Eid al-Adha, which means the "Festival of Sacrifices." Ashura honors the death of Hussein. He was an Islamic leader who died while fighting the ancient

Morning prayers during Eid-al-Fitr

A woman waves the Iranian flag on the anniversary of the Islamic Revolution.

Arabian empire in the 600s. National holidays include the Victory of the Islamic Revolution (February 11); Oil Nationalization Day (March 20); Islamic Republic Day (April 1); and the death of the Ayatollah Khomeini (June 4).

Sofreh-i Nowruz

Sofreh-i Nowruz is part of the Nowruz celebration. A large tablecloth is spread on the floor of the main room of a house. Then several important items are placed on it. First is a set of candles—one for each child who lives in the home. Once the candles are lit, they must be allowed to burn out on their own. Blowing them out would be bad luck. Another item is a copy of the Qur'an. It fills the air with goodness and hope for the coming year. Finally, seven food items are included. The name of each one must begin with the Persian letter *s*. A common one is a *sib*, which you may know better as an apple! Another is a clove of *sir*, also known as garlic. Each represents some part of the Nowruz celebration, such as health, love, and healing.

The Iranian flag has three horizontal stripes: green along the top, white in the middle, and red on the bottom. The green stripe honors the Islamic religion. The white means peace. The red is for the courage of the Iranian people. The phrase Allahu Akbar is written on the flag, over and over, in Arabic. It means "God is great." In the center of the white stripe is an emblem—four crescents and a sword. The crescents represent the Arabic word for Allah. The emblem also has the shape of a tulip. There is a very old belief in Iran that a red tulip will grow on the grave of any soldier who died while fighting for his country.

The basic unit of Iranian money is called the rial. One rial is equal to 100 Iranian dinars. Ten rials also equal one toman. Iranian coins come in values of 10, 50, 100, and 250 rials. Paper bills come in values of 100, 200, 500, 1,000, 2,000, 5,000, and 10,000 rials. As of May 2006, one U.S. dollar equaled about 9,145 rials.

Count in Persian

English	Persian	Say it like this:
one	yek	yek
two	do	doo
three	seh	see
four	chahar	chai-HAR
five	panj	panj
six	sas	shesh
seven	haft	haft
eight	hasht	hasht
nine	noh	noh
ten	dah	dah

Glossary

bazaar (buh-ZAR)   A marketplace in Iran.

chador (cha-DOOR)   A loose robe that covers a Muslim woman from head to toe. Only her face and hands are visible.

dormant (DOR-muhnt)   Not active; quiet.

mosaics (moh-ZAY-iks)   Designs made by small bits of colored stone, glass, or tile.

mosque (MOSK)   An Islamic house of worship.

Qur'an (kuhr-AN)   The sacred book of Islam.

turban (TUR-buhn)   A long scarf wound around the head.

Fast Facts

Iran is the second-largest country in an area of the world known as the Middle East. Saudi Arabia is the largest.

Iran's capital city is Tehran. More than 12 million people live there. Tehran is located at the northwestern edge of one of Iran's largest deserts, the Dasht-e-Kavir.

There are three main types of land in Iran: plateaus, mountains, and lowlands. Iran's largest plateau, called the Interior Plateau, takes up about half of the country. Most of it is empty desert.

Iran's highest mountain is Mount Damavand. It is also a dormant volcano, and it is nearly 19,000 feet (5,791 m) above sea level.

The Iranian flag has three horizontal stripes of green, white, and red. The green stripe honors the Islamic religion. The white means peace. The red is for the courage of the Iranian people. The phrase *Allahu Akbar* is written on the flag, over and over, in Arabic. It means "God is great."

In Iran,
98 percent of the
people are Muslim and
2 percent are other religions,
including Christian
and Jewish.

The basic unit of Iranian
money is called the rial. Iranian
coins come in values of 10, 50, 100,
and 250 rials. Paper bills come in values of 100, 200, 500, 1,000, 2,000,
5,000, and 10,000 rials. As of May
2006, one U.S. dollar equaled
about 9,145 rials.

Iran's largest lake is
Urmia. It covers more than 1,750
square miles (4,532 sq km). Urmia's water
has so much salt and other minerals that
fish cannot live there. This also means
the water is undrinkable.

There is one
official language in Iran.
It is called Persian or Farsi. It is
one of the oldest languages in the world that
is still used today.

As of July 2006,
there were 68,688,433 people
living in Iran.

Iran's longest river is the Karun. It
runs for 450 miles (724 km) from the western
slopes of the Zagros Mountains to Iran's border
with Iraq.

Proud to Be Iranian

Shirin Ebadi (1947–)

Ebadi is a lawyer and civil rights activist, as well as the first and only Iranian and Muslim woman to win the Nobel Peace Prize. She was born in Hamadan, in Iran's northwestern region, before moving with her family to Tehran the following year. She began studying law in college in 1965, and five years later started a career as a judge. However, she quit after the Iranian Revolution of 1979, when the nation's new leaders decided female judges would not have as much power as male judges. She did not practice law again until 1992. During this time she took particular interest in the rights of women and children, and soon opened two organizations: the Center for the Defense of Human Rights and the Iranian Society for Protecting the Rights of the Child. For her work in this area, she was given the prestigious Nobel Peace Prize on October 10, 2003.

Ruhollah Khomeini (1900–1989)

Khomeini was the ruler of Iran from 1979 to 1989. His father died before he was a year old, and his mother died when he was a teenager. He studied the Qur'an so closely that he was given the title of *ayatollah* (gift of God). In the 1930s, he spoke out against Iranian leader Reza Shah

Pahlavi. He thought Pahlavi was taking too much of the Islamic religion out of the country. He was also critical of Pahlavi's son, Mohammed Reza Pahlavi, who took over as Iran's leader in 1941. Khomeini was sent to prison in 1963, then out of the country in 1964. Nevertheless, he continued to speak out against Mohammed Reza Pahlavi. In 1979, however, Pahlavi was forced to leave office. Khomeini returned and, within a year, took over as Iran's new leader. He wrote new laws based on Islamic law. He became ill in the late 1980s and died in 1989. Millions of his people filled the streets during his funeral.

Reza Shah Pahlavi (1878–1944)

Pahlavi was leader of Iran from 1925 to 1941. He was born in 1878. Both of his parents soon died, and he became an orphan. He was very smart and courageous as a boy. He chose a military career at about the age of fifteen, and soon he was in charge of his own group of soldiers. As a young man, he saw how poorly Iran was being run. So, with his military might, he forced the government out of power. In 1925 he became the nation's new leader. Under his excellent leadership, Iran built thousands of miles of roads, opened new factories, made more money, and created a better government. He also gave women permission to do things they never could before. In spite of all of this, he was forced from his position by Allied Forces in 1941 during World War II. He eventually moved to Africa, where he died in 1944.

Find Out More

Books

Cultures of the World: Iran by Vijeya Rajendra, Gisela Kaplan, and Rudi Rajendra. Benchmark Books, New York, 2004.

Enchantment of the World: Iran by Miriam Greenblatt. Children's Press, Connecticut, 2003.

Modern World Nations: Iran by Masoud Kheirabadi. Chelsea House Publishers, New York, 2003.

Web Sites*

Academic Kids

http://academickids.com/encyclopedia/i/ir/iran.html

CIA World Factbook

www.cia.gov/cia/publications/factbook/geos/ir.html

World Almanac for Kids: Iran

www.worldalmanacforkids.com/explore/nations/iran.html

*All Internet sites were available and accurate when sent to press.

Index

Page numbers for illustrations are in **boldface.**

About the Author

Wil Mara began his writing career in 1988 with a series of pet-care guides. He has since authored more than seventy books, including many educational titles for young readers. Further information about them can be found at his Web site, **www.wilmara.com**.